The Spicebox

As Anya and Shivum followed Mummy

into the store, they moaned,

"Not another shop, Mummy! This is such a bore!"

"Two minutes more, my darlings," she said,

"I just have one more thing to buy."

Just then something spectacular caught Anya's eye!

A gorgeous box, so shiny and bright,

filled with colourful powders

that shone in the light.

Anya peered into the box … only to see

a wondrous sight of great beauty!

"Oh, that's our newly arrived spicebox,"

the shopkeeper said.

Anya longed to have it,

she would hide it under her bed.

"Please can we buy it, Mummy?"

Anya began to plead.

Luckily, her birthday was next week,

and so Mummy agreed!

Colours, textures, smells and powders galore –

Anya knew the spicebox was magical for sure.

Red Chilli

"Is that red powder chilli?" asked Shivum.

"Aaachoo!" It made him sneeze!

Mummy exclaimed, "My dear!

Will you be careful with that, please?

Fiery like a dragon, daring and bold,

chilli is powerful and its story must be told. . .

Chilli powder comes from chilli peppers:

red, green and yellow.

Some peppers will make your tongue burn,

while others are mellow.

The small red ones we use to make chilli powder

are always spicy and hot –

that's why when we cook with chilli,

we use a little, not a lot!

Chilli powder can spice up curries,

stews and even dessert.

But remember, chilli must be handled with care,

or you could get hurt!"

Spicebox

Mehra & Heetal Dattani Joshi

This book belongs to:

....

Scholastic Children's Books,
Euston House, 24 Eversholt Street,
London NW1 1DB, UK

A division of Scholastic Ltd
London ~ New York ~ Toronto ~ Sydney ~ Auckland
Mexico City ~ New Delhi ~ Hong Kong

First published in 2016 by Scholastic India Pvt. Ltd.
Published in the UK by Scholastic Ltd, 2018

ISBN 978 1407 18155 4

Printed in Malaysia

2 4 6 8 10 9 7 5 3 1

Papers used by Scholastic Children's Books are made from wood grown in sustainable forests.

www.scholastic.co.uk

Contents

Chilli and chocolate is an unusual but wonderful combination dating back to the ancient Aztec civilization. Ask a grown-up to help you with this recipe – and don't worry – this dish isn't at all spicy.
A tiny pinch of chilli powder makes this chocolate mousse truly magical.

240 millilitres (ml) double cream

100 grams (g) high-quality dark chocolate broken into pieces (at least 50%–60% cocoa solids is ideal)

1 tablespoon (tbsp) caster sugar

A pinch of red chilli powder
(our super-secret ingredient)

2 eggs, separated – you will only need the yolks – ask a grown up to help you with this

'Handle with Care' Chilli Chocolate Mousse

 Takes 30 minutes   Serves 4

1. Wash your hands and put on an apron.

2. Ask a grown-up to heat half the double cream on a low heat, stirring continuously for 2–3 minutes. Don't let it boil.

3. Add the chocolate pieces and sugar. Stir well until melted and combined with the cream.

4. Add a pinch of red chilli powder and mix well.

5. Beat the egg yolks and slowly pour into the chocolate-cream mixture, whisking continuously. Cook for an additional minute.

6. Pour the mixture through a metal sieve and set it aside to cool.

7. Using an electric whisk or beater, whip the remaining half of the cream for a few minutes or until it forms peaks that stand up by themselves.

8. Carefully add the whipped cream to the cooled chocolate mixture. Fold or mix gently until well combined. Don't overmix.

9. Pour the mixture into 4 bowls and put in the fridge for at least 4 hours until the mousse sets.

10. Top with whipped cream, chocolate shavings or berries. Serve and enjoy!

    P.S. See if anyone can guess what the super-secret ingredient in your mousse is.

Mustard Seeds

It was their favourite time of day – jumping on the trampoline;

Anya and Shivum, up in the air, featherlight and barely seen!

"Come on in, kids, it's time to clean up.

Dinner is served!"

That was definitely Mummy's voice,

loud and clear that they heard.

"Oh wow," exclaimed Mummy.

"You two are bouncing just like mustard seeds!"

"What are mustard seeds?" asked Anya. "Is it something that we eat?"

"Yes," explained Mummy.

"They're tiny balls of spice that bounce wildly if dropped.

The seeds sizzle and jump in a hot pan, just like popcorn when it's popped!"

"How cool!" said Shivum. "Will they jump on my plate too?

Or in my mouth or in my tummy?"

"No, my little one," said Mummy. "Once cooked, they don't act so funny.

But they will make you feel happy inside,

and your food will be extra yummy!"

These pancakes, made with chickpea flour (gram flour) and vegetables, are flavoured with mustard seeds. They are a great energy-booster and can be eaten as a snack or light meal. Bouncy mustard seeds have mood-lifting properties, so this dish may even magically bring out some smiles on a gloomy day!

---

100 g chickpea flour (gram flour)

240 ml water

½ teaspoon (tsp) salt

A pinch of ground cumin

A pinch of ground coriander

A pinch of red chilli powder (optional)

50 g finely chopped vegetables (Shivum's favourite combo is onion, tomato and pepper, but you could try grated carrot, radish and baby spinach with grated cheese … feel free to experiment. Ask a grown-up to help with the chopping.)

2 ½ tsp ghee or butter

¼ tsp mustard seeds

'Happy and Healthy' Savoury Pancakes

🕐 Takes 20 minutes

🍽 Makes 2–3 large pancakes or 4–5 mini pancakes

---

1. Put the chickpea flour in a metal or glass bowl, add the water and whisk well for a few minutes.

2. Add the salt, ground cumin, ground coriander and red chilli powder and mix Let the batter rest for 10–15 minutes.

3. Mix the finely chopped vegetables into the batter.

4. Ask a grown-up to heat ½ teaspoon of ghee or butter in a small pan on a high heat, add the mustard seeds and watch them sizzle and pop.

5. Immediately transfer the sizzling mustard seeds into the batter. Stir well.

6. Ask a grown-up to heat a griddle pan or frying pan on a medium heat. Add 1 teaspoon of ghee or butter. When the butter starts bubbling, add in half the batter (if you are making large pancakes) and quickly spread around the pan, just like an omelette. You can also make mini pancakes or shapes by pouring the mixture into metal cookie cutters in the pan.

7. About 20 seconds after adding the batter to the pan, drizzle a teaspoon of melted ghee or butter around the edge of the hot pancake.

8. After 2 minutes, release the edges of the pancakes. As soon as they are golden brown carefully flip them over and cook the other side for 3 minutes.

9. Remove the pancakes from the griddle or pan and serve them warm. Pancakes can be eaten plain or with ketchup, tomato chutney or Shivum's favourite accompaniment, plain yogurt.

Turmeric

On Thursday when Shivum came home from school,

he had the sniffles and kept going "Aaachoo!"

"Don't worry," said Mummy, "I have the perfect cure!"

She ran into the kitchen to gather ingredients galore.

Mummy filled a pot to get some soup cooking

with little Shivum by her side, closely looking.

He was a curious little fellow …

then suddenly the soup turned yellow!

"What just happened, Mummy?" Shivum asked wide-eyed.

"It's a magic spice in the soup – one that will heal you from the inside!"

Turmeric is a spice that's yellow and bold –

and turns everything to a beautiful gold!

Later that night, tucked into bed in his room,

Shivum looked out at the stars and the moon.

He wondered if they too had slurped a spoon

of Mummy's soup with the magical spice!

How else could they shine so golden and bright?

But it's time to get some rest now, so we'd better say good night!

This soup is perfect for when you have the sniffles or are in need of something simple and comforting. Vegetarians can swap the chicken for tofu. But don't leave out the spices – they pack in flavour and immunity-building powers, especially turmeric, a miracle spice that not only turns everything yellow but also contains magical powers (antiseptic and anti-inflammatory properties) that help you feel much better.

1.4 litres (l) water

2.5 centimetres (cm) piece of ginger, peeled and thinly sliced

2 cloves of garlic, peeled

1 tsp whole black peppercorns (or a mixture of black, white or green peppercorns)

1 clove (optional)

1 bay leaf

1 small cinnamon stick

1 star anise (optional)

1 carrot, half coarsely chopped, half thinly sliced (for later)

1 celery stick, coarsely chopped

1 medium onion, cut into quarters

1 lemongrass stick, coarsely chopped (optional)

4–6 pieces skinless chicken drumsticks and thighs (optional)

1 tsp turmeric powder

1 tsp salt

½ courgette thinly sliced

150 g tofu, cubed (optional)

1 lemon

1 small sprig of fresh coriander, finely chopped (optional)

'Get Well Soon' Turmeric Soup

 Takes 45 minutes   Serves 3

1. Ask a grown-up to add the water, ginger, garlic and all the whole spices to a stockpot or saucepan over a medium heat.

2. Add the coarsely chopped carrot, celery, onions and lemongrass. Bring to the boil.

3. If you are making the soup with chicken, add it in at this point.

4. Add the turmeric and salt.

5. Boil for 5 minutes, then cover and simmer for at least 20 minutes or until the chicken is fully cooked and falling off the bone. Follow the same cooking time for vegetarian soup.

6. Ask a grown-up to use tongs to pull out the chicken pieces and shred them using a fork (you may want to let the chicken cool down a bit before doing this).

7. Using a sieve or colander, strain the soup into another pan.

8. To the clear strained liquid, add the shredded chicken (vegetarians could add tofu instead of chicken at this point). Add the sliced carrots and courgette (cut into pretty shapes if you like) and simmer, covered, for another 5–7 minutes.

9. Pour the soup into bowls (the soup may be served by itself or over boiled noodles or steamed rice). Squeeze lemon over it and garnish with fresh coriander. Slurp away!

Cinnamon

"Is it Christmas yet, Mummy?
When is it? I don't remember!"
"Not yet, my darling," said Mummy,
"it's only just September!
Father Christmas is on holiday,
and the elves are resting too.
You'll have to be patient,
there are still three months to get through!"
Anya felt very sad.
Why oh why was Christmas so far away?
Then Mummy had a brilliant idea,
"I know! Let's just pretend it's today!"
But how could it be Christmas
without Father Christmas or a tree?
"If you think it and feel it and smell it,"
said Mummy, "of course it will be!"
Smell it? wondered Anya.
Whatever does Mummy mean?
"It's the magic of warm cinnamon,"
said Mummy, "that smells like a festive dream!
We'll wear red socks and bake treats,
then our home will smell divine.
We'll wrap presents, sing jolly jingles
and it will be just like Christmastime!"

Baking pies, biscuits and crumbles flavoured with cinnamon is a magical way to make your home smell festive. This is the perfect winter dessert – super easy to make and wonderfully scrumptious!

2 large apples (or you could use pears, peaches or strawberries)

1 lemon

½ tsp ground cinnamon

1 tbsp caster sugar

100 g plain flour

80 g butter, softened

'Smells like Christmas' Cinnamon Apple Crumble

🕐 Takes 40 minutes   🍽️ Serves 4

1. Ask a grown-up to peel and core the apples, then cut the apples into thin wedges. Put them in a metal or glass bowl.

2. Squeeze the lemon juice over the apple wedges. Add the cinnamon and sugar. Mix well.

3. Arrange the apple wedges in the bottom of a greased baking dish (you could choose a 20 cm pie dish or square baking tray).

4. Preheat the oven to 180°C / Gas Mark 4.

5. In another bowl, mix the flour and softened butter with your fingers. It should resemble breadcrumbs (that's why it's called a crumble). Cover the apples evenly with the crumble mixture.

6. Bake the crumble for 20–30 minutes or until golden brown. Serve warm with a sprinkling of icing sugar or a dollop of cream or ice cream.

Black Pepper

"A bedtime story, please!" Shivum begged his sister.

"OK, just one." Anya sighed. "But you'd better listen up, mister!

Once upon a time, on a choppy blue sea,

sailed a one-eyed friendly pirate whose name was Jimmy.

One day, while sailing, he came across a beautiful land,

where he saw many farmers working hard with their hands.

'Arrr,' cried Pirate Jimmy, 'give me all your treasure!'

'Ohhh, Mr Pirate!' they cried. 'All we have here is black pepper!'

So Pirate Jimmy filled his ship with tonnes of pepper that day

and sailed along to new countries far, far away.

Everywhere he went, people heard about his pepper treasure –

they were eager to buy some and experience the pleasure.

Pepper, more precious than gold, was now in their land.

It would flavour their food that was mostly bland.

For his worldly adventures, Pirate Jimmy we salute!

His magical journey is known as the Spice Route!"

TREASURE

Learn about the famous Spice Route as you gobble up these patties. They offer a healthy dose of muscle-building protein and are super delicious. The addition of black pepper makes them a pirate's favourite! If you are using fish in the recipe, see the note below that explains which kind to use and how to prepare it. If you are vegetarian, you can swap the fish for grated paneer (cheese) or vegetables.

2 medium potatoes

For non-vegetarians: 200 g cooked fish, flaked (A boneless fillet of salmon, cod, or any other white fish. Depending on the fish, you can boil, poach or bake boneless fish fillets in the oven until fully cooked. Allow the fish to cool and then gently break it up into small flakes with a fork. You may also use a 200 g can of cooked pink salmon.)

For vegetarians: 200 g of grated paneer or vegetables (Grated courgette or carrots, peas and finely chopped baby spinach work well. Squeeze out any excess water from the paneer or vegetables using a paper towel before mixing them with the boiled potatoes.)

40 g fresh coriander, finely chopped

1 tsp salt (adjust to taste)

½ tsp ground cumin

½ tsp ground coriander

¼ tsp freshly ground pepper

2 slices of bread, crusts removed and cut into teeny-tiny pieces OR 50 g breadcrumbs (we like to use Japanese panko breadcrumbs)

2 tbsp coconut oil, ghee or butter for shallow frying

'Pirate Jimmy's' Peppery Patties

🕐 Takes 60 minutes

🍽 Serves 3 (makes 6–8 patties)

1. Ask a grown-up to peel and boil the potatoes on a high heat for 20–25 minutes until tender. Let them cool, then drain and mash them.

2. Mix the fish (or paneer/grated vegetables), fresh coriander, salt, ground cumin, ground coriander and freshly ground pepper into the potato mash.

3. Soften the bread using a few drops of water and add it to the mash (the bread should be just moist, not wet). The bread's job is to bind the patties so that they don't fall apart when frying. (You can use 50 g of breadcrumbs instead.)

4. Mix the fish-potato-bread mash well, making sure there are no lumps, but don't overmix or it will become gooey. Adjust spices and salt to taste. The mixture should be delicious at this stage even before cooking.

5. Separate the mash into 6–8 even-sized balls. Roll each ball in your hand and flatten it into a small flat patty. Each patty should be 5–7 cm in diameter. Pat firmly, especially around the edges and place in a single layer on a plate.

6. Chill the patties in the fridge for 15 minutes.

7. Ask a grown-up to heat a tablespoon of oil, ghee or butter in a frying pan.

8. With a grown-up, cook the patties, four at a time (or as many as can comfortably fit in your pan), on a medium heat. Cook for 3–4 minutes on each side or until a crisp golden brown. If during the cooking process the pan looks too dry, add a bit more oil, ghee or butter.

9. Transfer the patties to a plate lined with a paper towel to absorb excess oil.

10. Add another tablespoon of oil to the pan and cook the remaining patties.

11. The peppery patties can be served with vegetables such as peas and corn (with a little salt and butter).

Coriander

Granny was busy cooking some curry

when Anya came round in a bit of a hurry.

"Oh, Granny," she exclaimed, "it smells so nice in here!"

Said Granny, "That's coriander you're getting a whiff of, my dear.

Look, it's these little green seeds

that I roast and grind into dust.

For curry to be delicious, coriander is a must!"

"But these seeds are dull and boring," said Anya,

"they don't have that nice smell."

"The heat brings them to life," said Granny,

who knew her spices quite well.

Anya had an idea and quickly grabbed a handful of seeds.

"I will plant them in the garden, near the tall wispy reeds –

when the sun shines hot, the seeds will come alive,

just like Granny said!

And grow like Jack's beanstalk, way up over my head!

Then I can climb up into the sky, to a magical place –

where I'll see rocket ships and colourful planets

that live in outer space."

There are lots of curry recipes out there, but this one is super easy and quick to make! The best part is, you can put anything in this curry – chicken, vegetables, paneer, fish, prawns or boiled eggs … just pick your favourite and pop it in! Don't forget to note the difference between ground coriander and fresh coriander leaves.

P.S. Have fun and try using small cookie cutters to cut your vegetables into different shapes.

1 small onion

1 clove of garlic

1 tsp finely chopped ginger

1 tsp oil

400 g protein (boneless chicken, fish fillet, shelled prawns, boiled eggs or paneer)

OR vegetables (chopped aubergine, courgette, cauliflower, butternut squash, green beans)

1 lemon

1 tsp salt

2 tbsp (30 ml) plain yogurt

1 tsp ground coriander

½ tsp ground cumin

A large pinch of turmeric

1 tbsp (15 ml) tomato purée

3 tbsp (45 ml) passata

1 tbsp finely chopped fresh coriander leaves, for garnish

'Reach for the Stars' Kiddy Kurry

🕐 Takes 30 minutes (plus 30 minutes for marinating)
🍽️ Serves 2

1. Ask a grown-up to finely chop the onion and garlic and combine them with the ginger.

2. With a grown-up, heat the oil in a wok or frying pan and sauté (gently fry) the onion, ginger and garlic on a medium heat until the onion browns. Set aside to cool.

3. In a metal or glass bowl, add your chosen protein or vegetables. Squeeze the lemon over the protein (or vegetables) and add the salt.

4. Combine the cooled onion mixture with the yogurt, ground coriander, ground cumin, turmeric, tomato purée and passata. Stir and coat the protein or vegetables well.

5. Cover the marinade and let it sit in the fridge for 30 minutes.

6. Remove the marinade from the fridge and let it sit for 10 minutes.

7. Heat a wok or frying pan on a medium heat and pour in the marinade. Bring to a boil and then cook on low heat for 5 minutes, stirring very gently.

8. If the sauce is too thick, add a splash of water. Bring the curry to a boil again, cover, then turn off the heat and let the protein (or vegetables) steam for a few minutes.

9. Depending on the type of protein (chicken or fish) or vegetable you're using and the size of the pieces, the cooking time will vary – so keep a close eye on it and be careful not to overcook or undercook! Paneer and fish/prawns tend to cook very fast. Chicken takes longer to cook and so do most vegetables. It's very important that chicken and fish are cooked through before you eat them, so ask a grown-up to check.

10. Garnish the curry with chopped coriander leaves and serve with steaming hot basmati rice.

Cardamom

"Bang bang!" they heard.

Whatever is that noise?

Is it the carpenter,

making a new box for their toys?

No! The toy box was already made

and the carpenter had long been paid.

"Bang, bang!" they heard again.

Whatever is that sound?

Is it the drumming toy soldier

that's always lying around?

No! That toy is out of batteries

and doesn't work any more.

It can't be the toy soldier, that's for sure.

"Bang, bang!" What is that awful din?

Is it the neighbour knocking at the door,

trying to get in?

No! It can't be the neighbour – she's away.

She's gone off to Spain on a holiday.

"Bang, bang!" Whatever could it be?

Ohhh, it's Mummy,

crushing cardamom pods for her tea!

There are lots of different kinds of tea, from Indian chai tea to English breakfast tea. At tea time, cake is always the perfect accompaniment! This cardamom cake recipe is a great introduction to baking. Have fun playing with the cardamom pods and carefully breaking them open to discover the magical flavour and fragrance inside.

5 green cardamom pods

60 ml whole milk

175 g self-raising flour

3 medium eggs

175 g softened unsalted butter

175 g caster sugar

1 tsp baking powder

A large pinch of salt

240 ml whipping cream, whipped into stiff peaks (optional)

3 strawberries, chopped into thin wedges (optional)

'Shhh! Be Quiet for Tea Time' Cardamom Cake

🕐 Takes 40 minutes

🍽 Makes a 23 cm square or round cake, or 12 large cupcakes

1. Preheat the oven to 175°C / Gas Mark 4.

2. With a grown-up, carefully smash the cardamom pods open with a pestle and mortar (or the end of a rolling pin in a plastic bowl).

3. Place the smashed cardamoms into the milk in a saucepan and simmer for 5 minutes (do not boil).

4. Strain the cardamom milk through a sieve and leave to cool.

5. In a large bowl, add the flour, eggs, butter, sugar, baking powder and salt.

6. Gently whisk everything together for a few minutes until you have a thick, smooth batter.

7. Slowly pour the cardamom milk into the batter and mix it well.

8. Grease a 23 cm cake tin with melted butter, or line a muffin tin with 12 cupcake cases. With a grown-up, pour the mixture into the tin or cases and bake for 30–40 minutes for the cake or 20–25 minutes for the cupcakes, or until golden brown. Insert a cocktail stick or fork into the centre of the cake to test if it's done. If it is, the cocktail stick/fork should come out clean.

9. To decorate your cupcakes with butterflies, cut the tops off the cupcakes and then cut the tops in half to create wings. Spoon or pipe some whipped cream on to each cupcake and arrange the wings on top. Add a slice of strawberry for the butterfly's body.

Cumin

The family was at an Indian wedding, full of laughter and zeal –
after dancing and singing, they sat down for a meal.
The grown-ups sat separately, sipping their wine,
the little ones had their own table – everything was just fine.
Until suddenly…
"Waiter!" called out Shivum. "There are bugs in my rice!"
"Oh, I'm sorry, sir," said the waiter, "that isn't very nice!"
The waiter examined the rice while Anya shrieked and jumped away.
Said the waiter out loud, "Those aren't bugs, sir, there's just no way!"
"Then tell me, Mr Waiter, what exactly are they?"
"Oh no!" cried out Anya. "They're in the potatoes too!"
Papa came over and asked, "What's this commotion, you two?"
"Our food has bugs, Papa!" they both declared.
"Those are cumin seeds!" exclaimed Papa. "You mustn't be scared!
Cumin seeds are a flavourful, nutty little spice –
they make plain food like rice and potatoes taste super nice.
Cumin makes you strong and healthy, so you need not worry.
Plus it will help your tummies digest all that delicious curry!"

A yummy side dish for any meal or great for parties, these pepper bowls are super fun to dig into (look out for bugs!). Packed with flavour, this recipe uses both cumin seeds and ground cumin so you can see how one spice exists in different forms. Thanks to the magical flavour and digestive powers of cumin, your tummy will be happy to gobble up all the good-for-you vegetables that are hiding in the cups under all the delicious cheese.

2 tsp ghee or butter

1 tsp cumin seeds

200 g basmati rice

1 l water

1 tsp salt

4 peppers (of different colours)

4 tomatoes

2 cloves of garlic, peeled and finely chopped

A handful of baby spinach, finely chopped

50 g sweetcorn

A large pinch of turmeric

A large pinch of salt

½ tsp ground cumin

1 tbsp ketchup or tomato purée

50 g grated mozzarella

'What a Wedding' Cumin Pepper Cups

 Takes 45 minutes  Serves 4

1. Ask a grown-up to heat a teaspoon of ghee or butter in a heavy-bottomed saucepan or frying pan and add the cumin seeds.

2. Once the seeds sizzle, add the uncooked rice and sauté (fry gently) for 2 minutes. Then carefully add the water and salt and bring to a boil.

3. Let the rice boil for 4–5 minutes, then simmer for 10 minutes. Cover the pan, turn off the heat and let the rice steam for another 5 minutes.

4. While the rice is cooking, ask a grown-up to cut the tops off the peppers and remove the insides with a teaspoon so that you have clean 'cups'. You may need to cut the bottoms slightly so that they can stand upright. Be careful not to make a hole.

5. Ask a grown-up to cut each tomato in half and grate them using a box grater. Discard the skins.

6. Heat the remaining ghee or butter in a wok or frying pan, on a medium heat, and add the garlic to it. Sauté for 1 minute.

7. Add the tomato and stir. Cook for 3–4 minutes, then add the spinach and sweetcorn.

8. Add a pinch of turmeric, pinch of salt and the ground cumin, cook for another minute and then add the ketchup or tomato purée. Cook for another few minutes.

9. Heat the oven to 180°C / Gas Mark 4 or the grill to a medium heat.

10. Arrange the pepper cups on a tray lined with foil or greaseproof paper.

11. In the cups, layer the cooked rice and tomato sauce and top with a generous layer of grated mozzarella. Bake for 10–15 minutes.

Garam Masala

"What's your favourite spice, Mummy?" Anya asked her mother.

"Oh, definitely garam masala," said Mummy, "it's like no other!

Garam means hot and masala means spice –

it's a blend of flavourful spices that smell incredibly nice!"

"What's a blend, Mummy?" asked Anya, quite confused.

"It's a mixture," explained Mummy.

"When lots of different things are used.

Like a special fairy's potion that gives you wings to fly

or a beautiful rainbow whose different colours light up the sky."

Cinnamon, cloves, pepper and more –

garam masala is made up of spices galore!

What goes in the blend is often a secret, a real mystery,

but when good things get mixed together, something magical happens …

and the rest is history!

Shepherd's pie is an English dish loved by people of all ages across the world. Comforting and hearty, this dish packs in lots of protein and vegetables that will make you super strong and clever! The addition of aromatic whole spices makes this family friendly dish unique and extra flavourful. Have fun mashing the potatoes, stirring the ingredients and decorating the top of the pie.

3–4 large potatoes

2 tbsp butter, softened

100 ml milk

A large pinch of salt

1 tbsp ghee (or butter)

1 large onion, finely diced

2 tbsp carrot, finely diced

2 tbsp celery, finely diced

1 clove of garlic, finely chopped

1 bay leaf

1 star anise (optional)

1 small cinnamon stick

500 g minced lamb (substitute soya mince instead if you're vegetarian)

1 tsp ground coriander

¼ tsp garam masala

¼ tsp ground cinnamon

1 tomato, finely chopped

120 ml passata

240 ml water

1 tbsp melted butter

'Magic Masala' Shepherd's Pie

 Takes 45 minutes   Serves 4

1. Ask a grown-up to peel the potatoes and boil them for 20–25 minutes minutes until tender.

2. Once the boiled potatoes cool a little, drain and mash them. Mix them with 2 tablespoons of butter, milk and salt to taste. Set the mashed potatoes aside.

3. In a heavy-bottomed pan or frying pan, melt the ghee over a medium heat, and add the chopped onion, carrot, celery, garlic, bay leaf, star anise and cinnamon. Stir until the onion is browned.

4. Add the mince and break up the pieces. Stir and cook for 5 minutes.

5. Add the rest of the spices and salt. Cook for 2–3 more minutes.

6. Add the fresh tomato and passata. Cook for 2–3 more minutes.

7. Add the water, a little at a time. If the mince appears too dry, add extra water.

8. Preheat the oven to 180°C / Gas Mark 4.

9. Cover the pan and simmer the mince mixture for 10 minutes.

10. Transfer the cooked mince to an oven-safe dish and then spread the mashed potatoes evenly over the mince, using the back of a big spoon.

11. Using a pastry brush, brush the melted butter evenly over the top of the mashed potatoes and then make a design over the top, using a fork.

12. Bake for 25 minutes in the oven until the top is golden brown.

Namita divides her time between cooking, writing, consulting and chasing her preschooler around the apartment. A lifelong foodie, Namita has lived on four different continents and gave up a successful career in digital marketing to launch Indian Spicebox, a brand dedicated to simplifying Indian cooking at home while giving back to children in need. She has written a cookbook, created a clever 'Spicebox Kit' and teaches cooking classes in Singapore where she currently lives with her husband and son. Namita holds an M.S. in Integrated Marketing Communications from the Medill School of Journalism at Northwestern University, Chicago, United States.

Heetal is an artist and designer, who is happiest when she is in the company of her paints and brushes, or when she's tinkering around in the kitchen with her little master-chef daughter, Arianna. After ten years as an Art Director in advertising, Heetal launched Beetle & Bottle, her own design label of children's accessories and personalized art. Illustrating children's books lets her combine her passions for art and children's literature. This is her second children's book. She currently lives in Singapore with her husband and two children.